Praise

"I've known Meg Johnson's work for a few years, but not until now did I realize she's been sitting on a rickety folding chair in a corner of my buzzy brain, transcribing the flukey rants and loopy ferocities that all of us—all of us—are feeling right now slash all the time. Pick up this book and eat it, I mean love it, I mean eat it."
DANIEL HANDLER, AUTHOR OF *WHY WE BROKE UP*

"To enter Meg Johnson's poems in *Without: Body, Name, Country* is to enter a spiral staircase in a tower full of fun house mirrors: the language distorts the familiar into new but recognizable realities, sometimes wryly hilarious, sometimes hauntingly unsettling. The images in these poems will catch you like a trapeze artist, bending and contorting in wondrous ways. The poems explore the subject of girlhood: the speaker 'is forever entering a room. Inhaling the cusp of capture.' In prose poems and free verse, Johnson excavates the topography of the body, of illness and anxiety, of politics and patriarchy, lamenting, 'I guess I was supposed to be flattered because people said I was pretty. But it felt like a liability to me.' This liability of living in a body, gendered, fertilizes the landscape of all the imagery. Read this collection and marvel as different parts of you are 'lighting up like a pinball machine.'"
ANNE CHAMPION, AUTHOR OF *THE GOOD GIRL IS ALWAYS A GHOST*

About the Author

Meg Johnson is the author of the books *Inappropriate Sleepover* (The National Poetry Review Press, 2014) and *The Crimes of Clara Turlington* (Vine Leaves Press, 2015). Her poetry has appeared in *Hobart, Nashville Review, Painted Bride Quarterly, The Puritan, Sugar House Review, Verse Daily*, and others. Her nonfiction has appeared in *Bust, The Good Men Project, Ms. Magazine*, and others. She received her MFA from the NEOMFA Program and has taught writing at various colleges. She is the editor of *Dressing Room Poetry Journal* and has served as an external reviewer for University of Akron Press. She was recently writer-in-residence at Fairhope Center for the Writing Arts.

Her website is: www.megjohnson.org

Without:
Body, Name, Country

Meg
Johnson

Vine Leaves Press
Melbourne, Vic, Australia

Without: Body, Name, Country
Copyright © 2020 Meg Johnson
All rights reserved.

Print Edition
ISBN: 978-1-925965-42-1
Published by Vine Leaves Press 2020
Melbourne, Victoria, Australia

Pieces in *II: Diagnosis* are non-fiction and were written from the author's perspective. Names have been changed.

Cover design by Jessica Bell
Interior design by Amie McCracken

A catalogue record for this book is available from the National Library of Australia

For my nephew Elliott

I: Vaudeville

I Am a Midwestern Winter

I have a collection of space heaters.
My hair was expected to be black
like my father's. You were conceived
by a beach and a valium.

I say *I don't have the best
immune system.*

> (I have a yeast infection. I have canker sores.
> I have agreed to be a 31-year-old dog sitter.)

I grew up wearing a tutu
over snow pants.
Stephanie Tanner and Dawn
from Baby-Sitters Club, mythical
to me as centaurs.

I think about warm places. As I listen
to Josephine Baker sing Brazil
I could swear she says
where you put your ass in it.

Meg Johnson, Bitch

All the Meg Johnsons
would like to kill me,
and I, Meg Johnson,
would like to kill them.

Another Meg Johnson
can wear your dead body
draped over them
like a fur stole, but
it's not illegal because
you're both named
Meg Johnson.

Feminist Meg Johnson
and alt-right Meg Johnson
cancel each other out, so
why even Meg Johnson
anymore?

When one Meg Johnson
claims the work of another
Meg Johnson as their own,
this is classified as living
body murder.

What is the meaning of life?
you cry out before getting
distracted by a purse. How many
cheeseburgers will it take
to resurrect you?

You will never eat enough
cheeseburgers, and that's
the end of this poem.

I Am My Own Planet

I don't suffer from night terrors, but
if I ever do, I hope I scream out,
Neely O'Hara! I could scream
this out while masturbating.

I'm masturbating for Mormons.
They can't, so I do it for all of them.
Let the record state, I am not
a Mormon. It's not that I'm against
religious freedom, just sexism,
racism, and homophobia. I could make up
some imaginary planets, but
I wouldn't consider it holy.

I'm surprised I don't have night terrors.
I have PTSD from when I had
Guillain-Barré. Guillain-Barré
is French for Old Man's Disease.
You now owe me five dollars
for the French lesson.

Sasha Velour as Joan of Arc

Her drawn-on eyebrows
will stay put with setting powder
until the blaze crawls up her body.

She had drawn herself with flames
at her feet in her sketchbook many times.

She first knew danger as a child.
She wore it like a stolen dress.

Precocious children are often alone.

Margaret said, *Give yourself*
to a desperate army. Become a woman,
a man, a sword, a mirror. Use every word.
Quickly.

Only portraits survive, so where
is that voice coming from?

She is forever entering a room.
Inhaling the cusp of capture.

Defiance to beauty to dust.

The Story of Menstruation

1
Have period sex and you will
likely conceive a monster.
You cannot properly churn
butter that time of the month.
You must stay in a hut, you must
curtsy with your back toward
the sun, you must roll around
on a sandy beach in a black
bikini in order to receive
forgiveness.

2
Fabric on a clothesline
flaps in the wind. *Red rag!*
yell the teenage boys
who run by. The girl
doing wash stiffens,
strokes the handle of
the knife at the bottom
of her wicker basket.

3
I take my lunchbox
into the bathroom.
I am eleven and a half.
The rule is bags,
backpacks stay in
the classroom during
the school day. So

my lunchbox becomes
a secret purse with
everything I need.

4
You must not speak about it.
Instead spread the blood
over a field of crops. Throw
menstrual cloths at unwanted
suitors. Laugh until you cry.

Sincerely

Dear A,

I'm sorry I had sex at your parents' house. I did not have sex with your parents. Unfortunately, they were home at the time. Not in the same room, of course.

It was probably rude of me to have sex with another man at your parents' as you staggered around the yard looking for a companion, ultimately failing.

The man was older. Different parts of his skin felt different ages.

I won't tell anyone about the orgy on the beach you participated in.

One of my students once asked me how to spell orgy. I said "Oh...um... I think it's o...r...g...y?"

A, I am not attracted to you, but I think you're handsome.

I'm not sure why you receive so many writing honors. You're a great writer, but so are a lot of people.

I appreciate that you're still a nice guy.

Sincerely,
M

Donald Trump, 75% Off

Press on Donald Trump's stomach
and it plays *My Sharona*.

When I was a little kid I thought
My Sharona was one word.
Possibly Italian for boner.

It was the era of Wayne & Garth
saying *Schwing!*

My Sharona isn't Italian for boner,
but the meaning of the song
still isn't great. Donald Trump can relate
to the song though because he loves
cruising for younger chicks.

If you lick Donald Trump's face
it is supposed to taste like an orange.
It smells like an orange, but tastes
like fried macaroni and cheese
left out at an aquatic center for
four days. The spoiled fried mac
and cheese is there to judge you
in your bikini. At least until
the raccoons eat it. The raccoons
are happy so there are some
happy creatures. God says
this meets the quota.

Instagram Envy

Women with platinum blonde hair, cream
colored sweaters, light tan pants, lie on beds
with white sheets, no blankets. Brunettes
wear thong bikinis, have their nails done, do
handstands. The redheads are slim with large
breasts. 1 in 4 people are vacationing in Bali.

It's been five years. You overslept again.

Style an overhead photo with a rope, a butterfly
wing, a plastic flower, a handgun, a lock
of hair, a padlock, one
mitten.

Post images of empty landscapes as
if no one has survived.

This Is Classy Because I Say So

I am staying at a house with a screened-in back porch.
It is not my house. I do not have a house. Let's all take a
moment to reflect on me being a single, childless, house-
less grownup. I know you want to.

(Pause.)

I ask if I can put an air mattress on the porch, make it
a sleeping porch. This will not solve my problems, but
will make my self-pity feel more romantic. I'm going for
vintage sadness.

(Time for questions.)

This New Normal

Blacking out
is curating
your memories!
But!
They say someday
we'll pay money
for time outside.
There will be a fee
to see the sun.

Wherever you go,
it smells like everything
is burning. Bells would ring
after every murder until
the last church was burned
down. The closest hospital
is three states away.

When your cell phone is on
fire, you try baking soda.
Your allotment of water is all
used up. The snow falls watery
and grey from the sky. No one
makes snowmen anymore.

You live in a house with fifteen
people. Being crowded doesn't
make anyone spatially aware.
The basement is full of bottles
of wine and first aid kits.

Everyone goes to city hall
every morning to see if
there is any work to be done.
Most days you get sent home.

The TV news anchor reports
government says, *Be patient.*
You no longer have access
to newspapers or the internet.
A housemate says, *Don't think
about the way things are
because you'll go crazy.* Then he
starts masturbating in front of you
and five others.

For years, stray dogs
and cats have followed
you as you walk home.
As you fish for your keys,
they lean against the door
hoping to be let in. Now
stray children follow you home.

Blacking out is curating
your memories. You have to
control something.

And for Perfume, I Use Shellac

I have so many goals in life. Like
performing the world's unsexiest
strip tease. I would start by posing in
a corn cob costume. I would peel off
my green layers to reveal my yellow
padded unitard. I would be dancing
to the Helen Kane song Dangerous
Nan McGrew. Maybe I should have
mentioned that first. *Hotcha, Chacha,*
Vo-doe-de-oh / And Boop-oop
Poop-oop-a-doop... Under fluorescent lighting,
I would look especially tired. The dark
circles under my eyes would accentuate
my eye sockets, highlighting the ephemeral
nature of life. Someone would throw a
teddy bear onstage and hit me in the head
with it. You would think they hate me.
But it's all part of the act! From seemingly nowhere,
I would acquire a pair of scissors, then cut off
the teddy bear head. I would lob the head
in the direction it came from, while gracefully
tucking the scissors away in the padding
of my corn costume. As I pull out handfuls
of stuffing from the bear's body and throw it
into the audience, I would continue lip syncing
to Helen Kane. *And I make a widow of a wife*
'Cause I'm dangerous Nan McGrew.

Grinding My Teeth

Don't you hate it when your imaginary boyfriend is mean to you? I've really built up a lot of resentment toward him. I found out he slept with an escort. Yes, it was before we met, and yes, he was single, and yes, he was overwhelmed with grief after his wife's death. It's totally understandable, but you expect me to be thrilled about it? That's crazy!

How did such a silly, bumbling old man even set up such an appointment you ask? His son set it up. My boyfriend's son is a very famous queer artist who supports the rights and dignity of sex workers, as do I, but come on. And isn't an Asian woman with breast implants a little too obvious? What about his son's deceased mother? Now that her soul is filled with vengeance, we can team up to kick ass. A human-ghost duo.

My boyfriend went to Europe without me. It was kind of a misunderstanding, I guess. When he invited me to go with him, I wrongly assumed he was paying for my flight. I guess he spent all his money on cardigans and that hooker. I'm really questioning what I'm getting out of this.

My boyfriend's name is Hans, but not really. I'm not going to tell you everything about him just because he isn't real. I told Hans about my real-life sexting buddy P and showed him a picture of P's big dick. He looked like a distressed gnome and said, *Are you trying to break an old man's heart?*

Someday I'll Love Meg Johnson

Even though she is a biological
woman who wants to be a drag
queen. Even though I read her diary
and she confessed
  Sometimes all you can do is laugh
at someone's ugly baby. And
  I held my warm heart in my hands,
surprised how easily I could function
without it. And of course
  I dated the Rust Belt.
It said I was a whore.
Different parts of me were lighting up
like a pinball machine when she said
  Jesus was not an Abercrombie
and Fitch model.
She once told me
  I would never judge you
for having an orgy, I would just
write about it. I watched
her body awkwardly flop
around in the style of Pee-wee
Herman as I tuned out the rest
of what she had to say.

      After Frank O'Hara, Roger Reeves,
      Ocean Vuong, Kyle McCord

Bat, Bat, Purse

My brother found a dead bat
in his dryer and did nothing.
The second time he found
a dead bat in his dryer
it was warm and crispy-like.
This bat he had tested for rabies.

A girl named Abby woke up
with a dead bat next to her
in bed. Her boyfriend at the time
was Nick. Nick's friend Sam
took the bat in for the rabies test.
Eventually Abby married Sam.

I gave some clothes, jewelry,
and purses I didn't want
anymore to a consignment
shop. When I stopped by
to pick up a check for my 40
percent of whatever sold first,

there was my old purse (from
an ex-boyfriend) on display
looking like new. Obviously
this isn't as gross as a dead bat,
but it still spooked me.

Tight

I was not a child
of product
demonstrations.

I would tie myself up
in string. Each tug
a prayer to be rescued
from the midwest.

I also wanted to be
a villain, but no one
knew this.

Shy children have the most
potential for danger.

I wanted a strapless top.
I wanted a new name.
A click in the dark.

A voice said, *Barter*
yourself. You were born
in a hallway. A stillborn
with a pulse. Exhaling,
the wrong place.

Mike Pence Watches Me Eat a Milkshake

The air conditioner buzzes, but
it's hot in the diner. A waitress
says he is here most days. He always orders
water and toast. He comes alone
and requests a booth that overlooks the tables
and the counter. I sit at the counter. His stare
confirms he is estimating my bra size.
He watches me alternate between
using a straw and a spoon. He starts mouthing
something at me. He seems to be mouthing
mother, mother, mother. I hope I'm mistaken.
In an untitled email to myself, I write
Never come back.

What is Male Entitlement?

Please give this poem a chance
even if you despise the title.
I love men. Most guys are superb.

This poem is not about a first-rate
guy. This poem is about my ex
boyfriend masturbating in the
woods and ejaculating on a tree.

Imagine the serenity of nature
and then *Once I was by myself*

out here and I was horny.
I walked up to this tree
and lowered my pants. It felt
great coming on the tree.

The bark transforms into
a sad pair of eyes, a head
in hands, a stone.

Thud

I'm a teenager in a night
time soap. I'm decades older
than I look. I spend all my free
time putting on lotion. It's just me
and lotion against the world.

I'm lucky my homework
is a prop. I need all the time
I can get to curl my hair into
perfect loose waves before
I disable a bomb.

Yesterday, I woke up in my trailer
to a man pointing a gun at me, saying
Get off my property.

Today, I was ready for a meet and greet
when a woman in a polo shirt and khakis
told me I must pay for everything
I eat. And to stop sitting in carts. I told her
I would call the network. She smiled
and said *Please do.*

I thought my life would turn
out better than this. My cheekbones
are practically vertical.

Betty White

Betty White, can I cry
on your shoulder?

My breasts are like
mood rings, they
already understand.

I want to wear a mood
ring as an adult
and not feel ashamed.

I want a thick friendship
bracelet long enough
to cocoon myself in.

I want to hide in the
dark with VHS tapes.

Somewhere there is
a twin bed who knows
who I really am.

II: Diagnosis

When in Doubt, Put on More Makeup

If I had lived during the Victorian era, I would have ended up with lead poisoning from piling on the period's dangerous makeup. Luckily, I was born in the 1980s. I received a Lil Miss Makeup doll as a gift. You could apply and remove her "makeup" with hot and cold water. I remember wondering why anyone would want to take her makeup off. Something was stirring in my little girl body. The beginning of a love story. An addiction, a language, a vow. On *Full House*, Becky said to D.J., "The secret to wearing makeup is to make it look like you're not wearing any." Even at a young age, I knew there were other ways to live.

On Growing Up Too Fast

By the first day of fifth grade, I was five-foot-five. My almost painfully skinny body made my A-cup breasts look much larger than they actually were. In a photograph in the local paper, I was in a dance costume with some other girls. "Meg had the biggest boobs in the paper," a classmate said during recess. I got my period in fifth grade at age eleven. I didn't tell any of my friends.

I could feel a shift starting in fourth grade. Strangers asked me if I was in middle school. Other girls loved and related to Shirley Temple. I couldn't relate to Shirley Temple at all. In upper elementary school I loved Isadora Duncan, Gypsy Rose Lee, Etta Place, Billie Holiday. I loved modern dance and studying Duncan was a gentle guide toward womanhood. With my dark hair, pale skin, and loose-fitting dresses, I could have been mistaken for a 1990s version of one of the Isadorables.

Gypsy Rose Lee felt like an archetypal role model for a physically mature young girl. Right away, I could identify that I was not a Baby June type. Baby June was Lee's younger sister and a Shirley Temple type in Vaudeville before Shirley Temple actually existed. Maybe it was odd for a young girl to relate to a Burlesque stripper and read so much about her, but at least I learned to embrace the womanhood that was thrust upon me.

Growing up in a college town was a source of relief. In a sea of college students, I was just another attractive young woman, not the spectacle I was around kids my own age. Especially when dancing, in costumes, made-up. People would say things to my parents like, "Better lock up your daughter. She's too tall and too pretty," and "They broke the mold when they made her." I overheard some of these comments, while my mom told me about others. I guess I was supposed to be flattered because people said I was pretty. But it felt like a liability to me. A dangerous burden. Something that could go wrong. A toddler with a loaded gun.

Some of my friends played orphans in a production of *Annie*. Backstage, I walked by Miss Hannigan, who was significantly shorter than me. "Why didn't you audition, Meg?" someone's mother asked me.

I tried not to think about attention I received from grown men. When a teenage boy would hit on me, it was intimidating, but at least it was less perverted. I could almost feel normal. I had an elementary school teacher who would call me at home like the boys in my grade, among other strange behavior. If my parents hadn't been so involved, I might not have been protected from this man who continually tried to force his way into my life until I physically left the state after high school.

At age eleven, I was staying at a hotel with my family for a relative's wedding. Walking through the hotel with my mother trailing behind me, a group of bikers leered at me. One separated from the group and moved toward me, saying "Hey. How are you doing?" My mother audibly gasped, and rushed forward to clutch me by the shoulders. "Who are you? Her bodyguard?!" the biker said to my mother, not concealing his anger. We walked past them (quickly, silently) with my mother still gripping my shoulders even though I was taller than her. My mother was forty at the time, possibly younger than the biker. Now that I'm over thirty, I realize that my mother wasn't that old herself.

My mother later told me about getting her period at age ten. Before that, she said, she could run faster than all the boys in her grade. Maybe she still could have outrun them. We'll never know. But given the realities of menstrual products in the '60s, who would want to try?

My childhood was over before I even knew it was ending. I watched many of my peers enjoy a certain freedom until high school. A childhood friend of mine didn't get her period until she was fourteen. I wondered what it was like for those girls. To have those additional years under the radar. I still wonder.

Breasts

I have felt bad about how my breasts look. Not because I think they're too big or too small. They aren't saggy. They aren't lopsided. Still, the current standards of beauty scream that my breasts are not right. The skin on my areolas has some variation in color. Some of the skin is a light pinkish brown you would expect, but some of the areola skin is white. White like snow, not the flesh color of my skin. Vitiligo causes skin discoloration, often small white patches. Vitiligo skin changes over time which is part of what makes it such a mysterious and isolating disorder. I found someone who did areola tattooing. Areola tattoos are usually done for women having reconstructive surgery after breast cancer. The esthetician explained that the process of numbing my breasts would be extremely painful for me because I had full sensation in my breasts, unlike women after reconstructive surgery. A nurse stuck a needle in each areola about half a dozen times, moving around the nipple in a circle. I had braced myself for the stab of the needle, what I was not prepared for was the pain of the injection in my body. The substance made me feel as if my breasts were being burned from the inside out. The esthetician did the tattooing and told me I could come in for a free "touch-up" a few months later. I never went back. The constant pain that followed the procedure for a week and the sporadic pain I experienced for months after shocked me out of my self-critical haze. The procedure didn't change the way I look very much. I'm not sure why I thought it would even work. I had tried putting self-tanner on my areolas to even out the color when I was younger and the skin wouldn't absorb it. There's a part of me that likes that the areola tattooing didn't work very well. Whenever I try to conform it doesn't take.

Guillain-Barré, 2016

My regular doctor sent me away and told me to come back if things didn't improve. She did rule out other possibilities first. I had an MRI which showed I didn't have MS and a CT scan that showed I hadn't had a stroke. Weeks earlier an on-call doctor had told me I had a sinus infection. At that point, I could still move somewhat normally (I was stiff and achy), but I had already had tingling and numbness in my hands and feet for at least a week. "But my hands and feet are numb and tingling," I said multiple times as she held to her diagnosis of "sinus infection." I went to the emergency room twice. One ER doctor told me it was "just anxiety." He even mocked me, imitating how I slid my hands in and out of fists, how I sighed. I could barely walk. I told him about my autoimmune disorder (vitiligo) and history of autoimmune diseases (a former bout with Bell's Palsy). He again told me it was anxiety.

Falling

I could only get upstairs by crawling. I had to hold onto something in order to walk. I had fallen down multiple times. "It has to be Guillain-Barré or Fibromyalgia," I told my mom after researching online. "Or else I'm dying." The part of me that thought I would die without a diagnosis thought often of my brother's friend, Hunter. He had grown up on our street and had died a few months earlier in a hiking accident. He had been living in the southwest and had been very committed to social justice and worked for the Innocence Project. I had thought of him often since his death that fall. I felt I should be more like him, devote more of myself to others. It was a tragedy he died at twenty-six. The weeks following his death I kept making the same note to myself. *How do you avenge a mountain?* Hunter, who had so much left to contribute to the world, was gone. The idea of me dying young from an undiagnosed condition seemed logical to me. I remember struggling to walk and thinking, "If it's my time to go, then it's my time to go." Finally, another on-call doctor said he suspected I had Guillain-Barré and finally, after three weeks of Guillain-Barré symptoms, I was admitted to the hospital.

The Single Woman

My neurologist was a man around my parents' age named Dr. Miller. He might be a bit younger than my parents, but still a baby boomer. I laid quietly in my hospital bed as nurses brought in what was needed for the spinal tap AKA lumbar puncture. Dr. Miller was seated by the bed. "Is it hard being single?" he asked. I felt my eyes widen in shock. How did he know I was single? Maybe my chart said I never had been married. I was silent as I thought about what to say. "Sorry," he said, after a pause. I was still thinking about how to respond. I finally said something about dating being easier in cities. That Iowa consists of families and college students, single adults being the minority. I've moved around a lot and have experienced various regional dating differences. But asking me... Right before the spinal tap? And how did he know I was totally single? I'm not married, but I have an exhaustive list of ex-boyfriends, and hypothetically, I could have had a boyfriend at the time. And by time, I mean two minutes before having a lumbar puncture. Before asking about the presumed difficulty of my single status, Dr. Miller had asked if I planned to write a book. I told him for the second time that I had two poetry collections published by two different presses. "No," he said. "A real book. Like *Harry Potter*. Are you going to write a book like that?" The first time I had said the word *poetry* to Dr. Miller, he flinched and blurted out, "I don't know why anyone would read poetry." He did the spinal tap four times, saying my swayed back wouldn't round enough even when I contracted. He explained how to round my back to me half a dozen times, even though I had told him earlier I was a professional modern dancer for six years when he was probing me about my life. The first time he said "round your back," I told him my lower back was swayed. "You have a swayed back," he said repeatedly as if I had never said anything, and as if my body wasn't mostly paralyzed.

Risk

In the hospital I had to wear a bracelet with the words FALL RISK. I turned the bracelet so I just saw the word RISK. I like the word *risk*. There was a matching FALL RISK sign outside my room. Like the bracelet, it was bright yellow and larger than necessary, with a blocky black font. I fully understood that I was a fall risk, but couldn't help feeling insulted. I'm a millennial. I was a professional dancer. Even when I could barely stand up, the sign felt slanderous. I had to be attached to a heart monitor at all times due to my rapid heart rate which Guillain-Barré causes for some people. Even breathing was harder than usual. My lungs had to be tested multiple times a day, another possible complication. A fourth of all patients with the disease have serious issues with their lungs. I'm lucky I didn't have to be hooked up to a ventilator, I was close to needing one. After over a decade of moving around by myself and living in different cities and states, here I was at the hospital I had been born in. My second day in the hospital I had an EMG test also referred to as a nerve conduction study. After nearly ninety minutes of being shocked like a dog too stupid to learn to avoid an invisible fence, I found out the Guillain-Barré was axonal. This means the axons of the nerves are damaged, not the myelin which is more common. When the axons of the nerves (the nerves themselves instead of the nerve lining) are damaged, paralysis happens at an even faster rate. *Rare,* the doctors said to me without attempting to soften their voices. *Severe case.*

Are You Dying?

Guillain-Barré Syndrome develops when someone has a bad virus, but otherwise has mysterious origins. Only one in a hundred thousand get the disease (perhaps that number will raise slightly with the Zika virus) and it is more common in men and older people. Anyone can get it though and even after significant recovery, I still get choked up thinking about children with Guillain-Barré. There is a five percent fatality rate. When you have the disease, it is hard to hear *five percent*. All that registers is *fatality rate, fatality rate, fatality rate*. When you have it, it's easy to imagine yourself dying from it. The dilapidation is real and rapid, and it's hard to believe your body will be able to recover at all. Most people do make a full recovery, but it can take months, years... Some are left with some of the paralysis and/or pain, some relapse, and others develop the chronic form of the disease, CIDP. Many suffer from chronic fatigue long term. Some suffer from depression and anxiety, some experience PTSD.

WaveRunner

What bacterial or viral infection did I have that led to this? There is more than one possibility. Perhaps even being sick multiple times created some monster virus, I don't know. In late January, I threw up in a date's car. A few hours later, I felt better, but I hadn't had that much to drink. It was violent projectile vomiting, and it was a first date. I should have been horrified. But the truth is, I've gone on so many bad dates that I felt relieved. Relieved that for once I was the bad date. I felt another kind of positive emotion. Pride? I've been dating for seventeen years. I feel that I should get something for this. A prize or present to acknowledge my effort. Even something I don't want, but could sell for cash, like a jet ski. After the violent throwing up episode/date I was in Minneapolis, and then Madison, Wisconsin for about a week and a half total. I felt okay, but had low energy. Then I went to Ohio to do some guest teaching at a college and give a reading. I felt as if I was losing my voice, but no one seemed to notice. My health deteriorated as soon as I got back to Iowa from Ohio.

Professional

I was supposed to go to New York and give two readings while I was in the hospital. I was shocked that I couldn't leave to do the poetry readings. I shouldn't have been shocked. I needed almost constant supervision. Still I couldn't wrap my head around it. It was my first time in my entire life I was missing a performance or reading. When I was in a dance company, I performed a series of shows on codeine and muscle relaxants. When I wasn't onstage, I was wearing a neck brace. I'm not saying that this was a good idea, but to me it seemed totally normal. The New York readings were scheduled on a Thursday and a Friday. Up until that very Thursday I kept asking everyone, "Do you think I'll be able to go to New York?" I had already told the curators of both reading series I was in the hospital, but I didn't quite believe it even as it was happening.

Grace

The physical therapist had me walk around the hallway. First, I had to put on a second gown to cover my backside. Then she secured a large black belt around my waist. Before each walk started, she would grab ahold of the belt at the small of my back which she continued to hold onto until the walk around the floor was finished. I felt like a circus bear being transported from the truck to the tent. I don't know if this is how circus bears are actually transported, but I can totally imagine it. My steps were awkward and birdlike. When I knew what stretches to do, the physical therapist asked if I do yoga. "...Sometimes..." I responded. I couldn't bring myself to say that I used to be a dancer, a dance teacher, a Pilates instructor... A second physical therapist started to work with me. When I did more reps than she asked for, she asked if I was in sports growing up. "...Umm, no... Dance..." I said shyly.

Scent of Another Woman (Or Man)

I had five days of IVIG treatment in the hospital which basically means I was hooked up to an IV with plasma for hours at a time. I smell like a stranger to myself. Actually, to be more specific, a collection of strangers. The IVIG treatments and lingering effects have made my own natural scent disappear or at least temporarily hide out. When I sweat I smell like someone else's B.O. Even when I'm cold and my skin is overly dry, a scent is seeping out that is completely human, but not at all my own. The first three weeks I am out of the hospital I continue to smell like other people. A different person every day.

Super Tuesday
and Other Primaries

I had to have a shot in my stomach every night to prevent blood clots, and I could see the dread and pity in the nurses' eyes before giving me the shot. One nurse accidently stuck one of my multiple IVs directly through a vein. Even though it was painful, she was too sweet to hate. A young male patient tech would dash in every time I pressed the call button. He worked in the middle of the night and he at least appeared to enjoy working at that time. I wasn't allowed to walk from the bed to the bathroom without someone watching me. The bathroom was only about six feet away from the bed. The first few days I protested, "I'm okay on my own," but every time I was shut down and told I needed to call for someone. All the patient techs and nurses would watch me walk to the bathroom and then close the door behind me. The young male patient tech would always close the bathroom door without it latching all the way. I was mortified. I felt too young for all of this. After reading more on Guillain-Barré, I discovered I was lucky I could tend to myself in the bathroom with my barely, but partially, working hands. One late afternoon when I was lying in bed, a nurse turned to my mom and said, "She's so pretty." It was the way someone talks to the parent of a child. I guess for all intents and purposes at that moment I was. In the hospital I got into the habit of watching MSNBC because what else is there to watch during the day? There was a commercial where a young man and a young woman ran up porch steps. I wondered if I would be able to do that again. I wondered every time I saw the commercial. There was also a commercial about addiction specialists featuring drug addicts' confessions. I remember thinking I would prefer an addiction to Guillain-Barré. I remember feeling actual contempt for addicts, even jealousy.

Adjunct Nation

The three previous semesters I had taught at a local
university as an adjunct. An adjunct's lifestyle is like
being a used tissue dropped on the ground and then
kicked at by a dirty shoe. One day a patient tech asked
me if I wanted players from the college football team to
visit me. I said no. "Some of them might be her former
students," said my mom, who had popped in for one of
her frequent visits. I wanted to tell the patient tech about
the long days of conferences I would have with composi-
tion students. Many of them would not bring their drafts
to conference for feedback which was the whole reason
there were conferences. Before each long conference
day, I would listen to the Nicki Minaj song "I Am Your
Leader" which includes the lyrics "I am your leader. Yes,
I am your leader. You're not a believer? Suck a big dick."
I wanted to tell the patient tech about that too, but I just
smiled and said, "I don't need anything. Thanks!"

Undressing on Command

I was finally allowed to take a shower when I could be approved to be off my heart monitor for a few minutes, but I hadn't fully thought it through. I hadn't thought about how I would have to be naked in front of strangers and (even behind a closed shower curtain) monitored. When I dropped shampoo on the floor, I couldn't pick it up. Someone had to hold my underwear for me to step into when I was dry. A month later when I could close my eyes in the shower at home without holding onto anything for balance, I savored the moment, just standing with my eyes closed under the shower stream. Just hanging out.

The Single Woman 2

Before being discharged, the king of neurology, Dr. Bates came to see me. Dr. Bates is past retirement age and has been at the hospital the longest. Sometimes he writes for the local paper. "I love your column," my mom said while sitting on the couch next to my bed. "Are you married or single?" asked Dr. Bates. I said single and then he scowled. "I'm going to go to my parents' house and my mom is going to take family medical leave for a while," I explained quickly, as if I was the last single person in all of North America. His facial expression suggested he found my recovery plan and life choices only mildly acceptable. I did some of the strength tests I had done with the other doctors. He cheerfully congratulated me on my progress and left. Later a nurse brought me my discharge papers and I was finally free of the heart monitor and IVs.

At My Parents'

I was still stumbling around a bit the first few days out of the hospital so my mom insisted I sleep in my parents' room since it's close to a bathroom. My parents slept in my brother's old room. I felt ridiculous, but was still having bad headaches and body pain, and the bed was really comfortable so... I thought of Regina George in *Mean Girls* making her parents trade bedrooms with her because it's the bigger room. My dad wanted to know when he'd get his bedroom back. My mom said not for a while. I thought of Amy Poehler as the enabling mother in *Mean Girls*, excitedly taking pictures of Regina in her skimpy bunny costume, and I thought about the father with his disapproving and baffled expression. I had panic attacks. I managed to not have one the day I gave a reading and did a Q & A at a college thirty minutes away. A person not physically appearing sick or stressed is not an indicator of wellness. I was still struggling physically, with movement, strength, and pain. I was on several medications. The pain made me emotional. All the medical sources I read suggested therapy for GBS patients and survivors. None of the doctors suggested this to me. I found a therapist and saw her for six weeks.

Beats Galore

Growing up, I was never very interested in superheroes and superhero origin stories. I was a girly teenager and an artsy girl, usually lost in my own thoughts. After having IVIG, I started thinking more about superheroes. I thought receiving IVIG for Guillain-Barré would make a good superhero origin story. After all, in real life, the treatment gave me strength, and I could literally tell through smell that what was going into me was human, but not my own. It didn't seem like a stretch that the IVIG could have accidently been mixed with something else, leading to a superwoman of sorts. I started listening to the *Bionic Woman* theme song. My regular physician was not happy that my heart rate was still up. My heart rate had been consistently average before the Guillain-Barré, and she felt something needed to be done about it. I went to a cardiologist. I was the only non-elderly person in the waiting room. I had an ultrasound on my heart, walked on a treadmill, then had another ultrasound. (Eventually I could run again, but still wasn't there yet that day.) My heart was functioning fine, but the heart rate was too fast. Permanent damage to the vagus nerve. I was put on a heart medication. I can never get a flu shot again or a DPT vaccine. The Guillain-Barré "souvenirs" were adding up. Soon I would be feeling a bit better and would then discover the chronic fatigue. The nurses at cardiology were very nice. As one smoothed gel onto me as I was lying on my side, I started thinking about Patty Duke. I thought about her in *Valley of the Dolls*, fighting to get out of the strait-jacket-bathtub thing by poking at a hole in the fabric with her toe. I saw this so clearly and wondered about Patty Duke and her life. As soon as I got home, I saw on the news that Patty Duke had died that morning. I felt sad, but not at all shocked. I recognize this as a coincidence, but I also like to think that my superpowers were starting to kick in, even if the superpower was only mild intuition. I thought to myself, half-jokingly, that the rest of my powers would kick in eventually. I was still in the discovery period.

The Single Woman 3

I had a new physical therapist for outpatient physical therapy. The first question he asked me was "Are you married?" "No," I said, not elaborating on my answer and letting an awkward silence grow.

Attack of the Texting Sister

I might not have kids. Since I've had Guillain-Barré syndrome, if I ever get pregnant, it would automatically be classified as a high-risk pregnancy. Sometimes women develop Guillain-Barré or Bell's Palsy while pregnant when they've never had either before. Sometimes women who have never had GBS before develop Guillain-Barré after giving birth. These are healthy women. Pregnancies or giving birth can trigger relapses for women who have had GBS or have the chronic version, CIDP, and can trigger a relapse of Bell's Palsy. And who knows what else could happen to someone with a high-risk pregnancy. During a panic attack, I texted both my brother and sister-in-law, who are already expecting their first child, that I want them to have "lots of babies. At least three." I explained the situation. I explained that on top of it all, "I don't know if I would ever have a supportive enough partner" to have children with, as a regular woman and especially as a woman with health issues. I texted that I "don't want to miss out on some life experiences so I want to be a busy aunt." They both responded to my texts speedily, reassuring me that everything will work out. Later that day, I wonder what's happened to me. My anxiety has made me crazy. I'm telling my sister-in-law what to do with her body as if I'm a Republican senator.

Hot Sick Girl

One of my first nights out of the hospital, an ex-boyfriend contacted me on social media. He said he was glad I was out of the hospital (that was all he said about my current situation) and then went on to tell me he would be in the area the following night. I knew what that meant. I didn't respond. Who tries to hook-up with someone right after they are discharged from the hospital and are still ill? Up until a few years ago, I sometimes gave into the ridiculous social pressure to look and act sexy as often as possible. This social pressure seems to be exclusively for girls and women and applies even when you are seriously ill. If you can't be healthy and sexy then be a hot sick girl, the world tells us. By ignoring my ex, I firmly said no to the pressure. (And of course, said no to this asshole ex-boyfriend.) It's all about healing for me. But I still felt society's pressure to be sexy again ASAP.

Recovery Diary

March 31
I was right. I'm even more anemic now because of all the blood they took in the hospital plus blood tests after being discharged. The specialist said so. Was only slightly anemic when admitted to hospital. Blood tests that were sent to Mayo Clinic come back okay.

April 3
Have been able to walk upstairs at a regular speed without holding onto a railing for a couple weeks. Still on various medications. Still several doctor's appointments every week. Can do twenty minutes on exercise bike and short walks. The hospital hasn't asked for payment yet. The clinic business office constantly hounds me to pay more than my monthly payment plan.

April 9
Forty-five-minute workout on exercise bike.

April 29
I'm so tired of people acting like you should hate yourself if you're not in *The New Yorker*. What are you supposed to do? Hold a gun to Paul Muldoon's head? You should accept yourself as a poet not in *The New Yorker*. I had to accept myself as a young woman going to the bathroom with an IV pole.

May 1
Two months and a day after being diagnosed, my feet still hurt off and on.

May 5
Worked out for an hour today. (Exercise bike.) Able to walk outside longer.

May 12
Last physical therapy appointment.

May 21
Can do a lunge, but uncomfortable in Pigeon.

May 22
Work out for ninety minutes. (Exercise bike.)

June 12
Orlando shooting. Continuing cycle of watching and reading the news and crying.

June 13
Still hurts to crouch down. Still need lots of sleep.

June 13
I wish I could report that everything is now amazing for me. In truth, Guillain-Barré has made a mess of my life, but I'm grateful I'm almost healthy enough to start to put it back together.

July
Nerves regenerating feel like rubber bands snapping inside your body.

August 3
My nephew is born. I act as if being back at the hospital isn't stressing me out.

2017
Second round of physical therapy.

2019
Full recovery is a relative term after Guillain-Barré Syndrome. My doctors consider me fully recovered because I can walk. I'm so glad I can, but I now live with extreme fatigue and nerve pain. My hands often shake. That's the abridged list of changes. I live in a different body now.

Women and Mortality

All we know is the country she was murdered in. We
don't know exactly why or how she died or who killed
her. We know it wasn't a suicide. She was a woman
in a foreign country investigating human trafficking,
so there are many possibilities. There are also many
conspiracy theories. There was no autopsy. Her body
was never returned to her family. They were not given
a cause of death.

*

A woman murdered in my mother's hometown. A woman
murdered in my hometown. If I have children, women
will be murdered. If I don't have children, women will
be murdered.

Final Note

So many shadows today. The beast of chronic pain. My almost three-year-old nephew following me everywhere. My actual shadow, inky on concrete. I believe in pancakes. I believe in naps. I am not sad about my sadness.

Acknowledgements

Thank you to the following publications, where pieces in this book originally appeared, sometimes in earlier versions.

Bear Review

Bust Magazine

The East Bay Review

The Good Men Project

Hobart

Maudlin House

MAYDAY Magazine

The Plot by Villainess Press

Print-Oriented Bastards

Role Reboot

Sprung Formal

Superstition Review Blog

Tinderbox Poetry Journal

Vending Machine Press

Vine Leaves Press

Enjoyed this book?
Go to *vineleavespress.com* to find more.

9 781925 965421